Mary Rose

Christmas 2000

Other Books by Ann Weems

Family Faith Stories
Kneeling in Bethlehem
Kneeling in Jerusalem
Psalms of Lament
Reaching for Rainbows: Resources for Creative Worship
Searching for Shalom: Resources for Creative Worship

Putting the *Amazing* Back in *Grace*

Ann Weems

Westminster John Knox Press
Louisville, Kentucky

Book design by Sharon Adams
Cover design by Pam Poll
Cover photograph © 1999 PhotoDisc, Inc.

First edition

Published by Westminster John Knox Press
Louisville, Kentucky
This book is printed on acid-free paper that meets the American National Standards Institute Z39.48 standard. ∞

PRINTED IN THE UNITED STATES OF AMERICA

99 00 01 02 03 04 05 06 07 08 09—10 9 8 7 6 5 4 3 2 1

Library of Congress Cataloging-in-Publication Data

Weems, Ann, 1934–
    Putting the amazing back in grace / Ann Weems.
        p.   cm.
    ISBN 0-664-22150-5 (alk. paper)
    1. Christian poetry. American.   I. Title.
    PS3573.E354P88   1999
    811'.54—dc21   99-23197

To David,
whose name says it all:
Beloved

–Mom

Contents

Introduction

I am a child of the Church. I use a capital C because I'm speaking of the Church beyond any particular congregation, and although my heritage is that branch of Christ's Church which is called Presbyterian, other branches swing in the same wind, the wind of debilitating discord and chaotic quarrelsomeness.

In recent church assemblies, I've witnessed church people "having at it," each side speaking in mean-spirited ways about the other, red-faced men and women raising their voices, pounding their fists on the tables in front of them, as they declared the opposing view was not Christian. Accusations are rampant, and name-calling flies back and forth across the Church of Jesus Christ! We are a divided Church, and in our divisiveness we have forgotten who we are and to Whom we belong. We've also forgotten our memory work: "Be ye kind one to another."

Of course, I'm aware it's not the first time the Church has lost its way, and you, the reader, are no doubt saying, "And it's not the last time, either." You're probably right: It's not the first time, and it's not the last time, but it is *our* time.

For years I've been haunted by Jesus' question: Who do they say that I am? In this time . . . in *our* time . . . what is it we are saying to the world about the One whom we claim to follow? Who do we say that he is? In the midst of all this infighting, do we dare to call him the Prince of Peace? In the midst of our bellowing, do we forget a world is out there, crying to the Church for help, crying in the name of Jesus?

There is a trend in the Church today for a congregation to write a mission statement. I'm stunned. The Church of Jesus Christ is two thousand years old, and we don't know what our mission is? Perhaps that's our problem. Each church seems to be a little kingdom, and a mission statement turns out to be what we want the church to do for us.

Have we forgotten to "love the Lord your God with all your heart and all your mind and all your soul" and "love your neighbor as yourself?" Have we forgotten who is in charge of the world and the Church? Have we forgotten to go into all the world and preach the gospel? Have we forgotten what the gospel is? When we're throwing bad news at each other, the world will not hear the good news of Jesus Christ.

A few years back, all this fighting reminded me of children yelling irrational and unkind things at one another . . . but the children end up hugging each other and getting along just fine five minutes later. We're adults, and we're not getting along just fine, and it's been years. We seem to have forgotten who we are. No one says of us: "How those Christians love one another!"

I began to think about children and about how children learn about Jesus and God, and I remembered my own growing up and the quarreling that went on in the Church when I was a child. And then I remembered the grace of God. No matter what happened then and no matter what happens now, I am the recipient of the grace of God. It is utterly and profoundly freeing.

The grace of God is so profoundly freeing that we can disagree and hold hands at the same time. When we realize how much we have been given, we are no longer slaves to the agony of trying to be God to one another. We are no longer bound to the pile of rules we've made to bind one another. We are no longer bound to our insecure little kingdoms, thinking we have earned all that we have. Instead, we are free to live in the kingdom of God. We are free to praise God for the grace bestowed on us. We are so free, we can love one another in the beautiful loving spirit of Christ.

In this book, I went back to my childhood to think again about how I learned about faith. The more I thought about my childhood experience, the more I realized it was not about me. It was about receiving grace. Perhaps the Church can go back, go back in memory and relive the learning of our faith, and then go forward in gratitude for the grace that is ours.

The quarrelsomeness that plagues the Church today is not about how right these people are, and it's not about how right those people are; it's about our response to the amazing grace of God. It's not about choosing sides and continuing the fighting; it's about Jesus. It's all about Jesus . . . but we forgot.

The good news is that we can be forgiven. The good news is that the kingdom of God is not about what you want or what I want; it's about Jesus, the amazing grace of God. The good news is that once more we can together be the Church of Jesus Christ and turn our hearts to the world that cries for help in Jesus' name. Perhaps then the world will look at the Church and say, "Christ is the Prince of Peace" and "How those Christians love each other!"

Ann Weems

Mallard — Oh No ! etc.
Oh well, I can work with that !

PUTTING THE AMAZING
BACK IN GRACE

≫≫≪≪

My mother wrote fiction in the breakfast room;
my father wrote sermons in the study;
I wrote poetry in the maple tree . . .
that friend of a tree who gave me sanctuary,
hiding me in generous foliage from the voices
who called me to do homework or dishes . . .
that friend of a tree, who asked nothing, yet . . .
lifted me closer to the stars.
I'm not certain when I first
became enamored of words.
I suspect the fascination came
from the sound before the sight.
Our father and our mother filled our heads
with stories, both secular and sacred.
The words of nursery rhymes
and the words of psalms
embedded themselves within me.
Words . . . glorious words . . . ,
words memorized that live with me still,
words that come unbidden from shadowy
corridors connecting mind and emotions,
words that bring welcome meaning
to the present's moment.

Of course, the present moment finds the church
in chaos: splintered, fractious, quarrelsome . . .
an unpleasant place for poets.
The bickering drowns out the cries of the poor.
Our hearts are closed against the poetry of God.
And we are amazed about nothing.
Poets weep because we'd rather be
out searching for stars.
So the question is: What's a nice poet like me
doing in a church like this?

I was born and bred in the Presbyterian briar patch.
I was one of those children who actually
wanted to go to Sunday School.
By the time I was six, I was completely
captivated by the Red Letter Testament.
I read it in my tree.
I read it in the red leather chair
in my father's study, and by flashlight
when I should have been asleep.
Beautiful red letters . . . Beautiful red words . . .
out of the mouth of Jesus. . . .
"Jesus loves me, this I know
for the Bible tells me so."
"Let the little children come unto Me."
So we came, dressed in our best for Jesus,
our nickels clutched in our hands,
our little souls waiting for the Spirit,
our little hearts already given away . . . to Jesus.
We gladly put our nickels in the hand of Jesus.
We knew what the red words said:
"Feed the hungry."

Jesus took our nickels and bought food
for starving children all over the world.
We had learned that
"the Lord loves a cheerful giver."
We gave, and we were cheerful about the giving.
Soon, however, I noticed that not everyone
who went to church was cheerful.
I noticed it, but I didn't understand it.
Didn't they have Red Letter Testaments?
And why were they mad at my father
because he preached about peace?
And why did their faces turn red
when he preached about racial equality?
And why did the angry phone calls
come when he preached against
low wages for the poor?
Why did people make faces
when he preached about loving
people of other faiths?
They said don't preach about poverty,
and don't preach about peace, and
don't preach about loving other people,
not if their skin is another color,
not if their faith is not called Christian.
I was confused because I had
memorized these red words:
"You shall love the Lord your God
with all your heart and with all
your soul and with all your mind.
This is the greatest and the first commandment.
And the second is like it:
You shall love your neighbor as yourself."

If the first commandment is to love the Lord
your God with all your heart, soul, and mind,
and if the second is like it,
then the way to love God is to love
your neighbor as you love yourself.
I figured it out: I didn't love God if
I said something mean to Norvella,
whose skin was black.
I didn't love God if I wouldn't
let Jerome Rosenfeld play with us.
I didn't love God if I wanted to
bomb the Germans, and I didn't love
God if I didn't share my money.
My father said there was something else.
He said he didn't love God
if he didn't love the people who
wouldn't share their money.
He didn't love God if he didn't
love the people who hated Norvella.
He didn't love God if he didn't love
the people who hated Jerome Rosenfeld.
He didn't love God if he didn't love
the people who wanted war.
He didn't love God if he didn't love
the people who were calling him names,
the people who were trying to get rid of him,
the people who did get rid of him.
Then he said he didn't love God
if he didn't forgive them, and
he didn't love God if he didn't
try to reconcile with them.
I didn't know what "reconcile" meant,

but my mother said it meant that
Jesus forgave the people who nailed him
to the cross, and he loved them still.
That sent me to the Red Letter Testament.
Sure enough, in red words Jesus says:
Forgive them, for they don't know
what they're doing.
It was the most astounding thing I'd ever heard!
Forgive the people who nailed him to the cross. . . .
Forgive the people who despised him.
Forgive the people who rejected him.
Forgive the people who denied him.
Forgive the people who abandoned him,
the people who left him all alone.
Forgive the people who nailed him to the cross.
Because of that, my father was supposed
to forgive and love still
the very people who called him names,
the people who turned his life upside down,
the people who told him he wasn't
the kind of preacher they wanted.
I began to feel a little guilty,
because to tell you the truth,
I was mad at Norvella
because she was so bossy,
and as a matter of fact,
I was tired of Jerome Rosenfeld
hanging around all the time,
being so cheerful.
And what was I going to do
to stop that tune from whirling
around in my brain: "Praise the Lord

and pass the ammunition"?
At least I liked giving my money
to Jesus for the starving children,
but I didn't know how far
that was going to get me.
So I wrote a poem, an adjective-laden poem,
about how much I loved Jesus.
I showed it to my mother,
who warned me about being pious.
My mother said she abhorred piosity.
Of course, I didn't have any idea
what that meant.
My brother said it meant she hated
people acting so goody-goody.
"You don't want to be like the Pharisees,"
she said.
Pharisees. . . . What a delicious word!
Pharisees. . . .
But when I found it
in the Red Letter Testament,
I was horrified. Was I a Pharisee?
My own mother had warned me!
Even Jesus was mad at the Pharisees.
I tore up the poem.
All those beautiful adjectives
ended up in the wastepaper basket.
That was just the first time.
When we moved to our new home
and our new church, I felt better.
We had escaped from the Pharisees.
In 1942 I joined the church.
I was eight years old.

When I said Jesus Christ was my
Lord and Savior, something happened
in my little eight-year-old heart.
I was astounded at my good fortune,
amazed that, even though I had Pharisee
tendencies, I could join this church
where these people wanted to hear
my father preach about peace and race
and justice for the poor and co-operating
with people of other faiths.
I was nurtured by this community of faith.
The Presbyterian Church became my home.
About this time I read in my Red Letter Testament
the story of the woman who touched the hem
of Jesus' robe and, because of her faith, was healed.
I wondered why we had to go through
all that quarreling in the other church,
and why I had to be so careful not to be
a Pharisee, when all she had to do
was touch the hem of Jesus' robe.
My father said it was a matter of faith.
He said we were all inheritors of this faith.
It was something like inheriting Great-
Grandfather's money, which we didn't,
but . . . we did inherit our faith.
My father said that God had given us far more
than Great-Grandfather ever could have given.
God had given us Jesus, who calls
the whole world to his table . . .
Jesus who forgives, and loves us still,
even when we, like sheep, have gone astray . . .
even when we despise and reject him,

even when we abandon him. . . .
Over time, I realized that my father
had forgiven the red-faced people
who called him names.
When we saw them on the street,
he would greet them cheerfully.
I could tell he loved them still.
I thought it was amazing!
I prayed to Jesus not to let me grow up
to be a Presbyterian Pharisee.
My mother, the writer and the lawyer,
pointed out that the people who Jesus
chastised were the good church people,
the ones who claimed that they,
and they alone, knew the real truth,
the ones who knew the letter of the law,
but did not act in the spirit of the law.
My father called them hard-hearted.
He said there's no reason why
Christians can't disagree
and hold hands at the same time.
Now, isn't that amazing!?

I attempted another poem.
My mother said that it was better,
but maybe I'd like to go with her
to a writing class. I did and this time,
I tried a poetic short story.
The teacher said it was a perfect
short story, as soon as I scratched
out all the lovely adjectives.
What a temptation it is to string

pretty words across a page and call it poetry.
What a temptation it is to think that
my little kingdom is the Kingdom of God.

I was warned years ago that nobody likes
poetry and certainly nobody buys it!
What worried me then, what worries me
still, is how easily we in the church
forget the poetry of God,
how easily we in the church
extract the amazing from grace,
how easily we turn
Hosanna into ho-hum and
belief into bureaucracy and
righteousness into rules.
Addicted to our agendas,
bound to our budgets, we fail to
remember that the Love of God
is written upon our hearts . . . ,
not in the Book of Order.
When we worship process,
we obliterate poetry.
We cover our eyes and our ears
against the beautiful red words,
the amazing words of the Word.
Jesus told the people to love their enemies,
and the people were amazed.
He told them to have compassion for strangers,
and the people were amazed.
He overturned the tables of the moneychangers,
and the people were amazed.
He told them to pray for those who persecuted them,

and the people were amazed.
He told them to set the captives free,
and the people were amazed.
He broke the rules, and healed on the Sabbath,
and the people were amazed.
While we in the church are spending
our energy on arguing,
who will bind the wounds?
And who will free the oppressed?
And who will feed his sheep?

I'm back in the church down in Tennessee. . . .
Yes, yes, I know: The Presbyterians have
a history of fighting . . . , but our faith has a
history of forgiving.

I have reached for rainbows.
I have searched for shalom.
I have shared my family faith stories.
I have knelt in Bethlehem.
I have knelt in Jerusalem.
I have cried my laments in the face of God,
and God has continued to leave
stars where I can find them.
Surely, we in the church have love enough
to disagree and hold hands at the same time!
"He was despised and rejected,
a man of suffering and acquainted with grief."
Who do we say that he is?
Who do we say that he is by the way we live?
"He is the One who was wounded for our
    transgressions.

By his bruises we are healed.
By his punishment we are made whole."

I don't know how we ever got so unamazed,
but the amazing thing is: Even now
Jesus speaks the poetry of God.
Even now we can touch the hem
of his robe and be healed.
Even now we can share our bread
and our wine with a starving world.
Even now, God the Poet pours grace
upon our heads like snow on snow on snow.
Even now we can be amazed!

PLANTING SEEDS

❧❧❧❧

My father's wheelbarrow
was filled with children.
Jostled and laughing,
we bumped along to the garden,
where we were taught to plant.
The first thing we learned
was to get on our knees.

The man who came to see my father
wasn't smiling when he said hello.
He and my father sat in the study
for more than an hour.
We waited in the wheelbarrow.

True to his promise, our father
took us to the garden, where we
got on our knees and planted seeds,
even though our father said
we might be living somewhere else
when the flowers bloomed.

My father said there were people
in the church who didn't want him
to preach about peace

and racial equality
and higher wages for the poor.
These people told my father
to stick to the Bible.
Uh-oh, my brother said.
So I said it too.
Uh-oh.

Sometime later the voting began.
The Session voted to take
the matter to Presbytery.
The Presbytery voted that
my father should resign
for "the unity of the church."
The Synod voted that my father
should not resign because he was
a righteous man who had preached
the gospel of Jesus Christ.
The congregation voted "overwhelmingly"
that they wanted my father to stay.
"Overwhelmingly" meant most,
but not all.
My father said it was those few
that worried him.
Contentiousness had been planted, he said,
and it was growing like a weed.
Uh-oh.

My father resigned because he didn't want
to spend his ministry on quarrelsomeness
when there were so many matters
of justice and mercy in this world,
so many people who needed

the compassion of the Church.
Besides . . . he was tired of all the voting . . .
as though we in the Church could vote
people in or out of the Kingdom of God.

My father's wheelbarrow belongs to my brother.
He fills it with laughing children
and takes off for the garden
to teach them how to plant.
The first thing they learn is
to get on their knees.
The harvest belongs to God.

THE HOSANNA WOMAN AND
THE THANK-YOU MAN

❧❧❦❦

My sister and I divided the stars
on a warm June evening down in Tennessee.
Then little by little . . . for trinkets and favors . . .
she traded her stars until I owned the sky . . .
well, God and I; we owned the sky.
It was years before I learned
that stars are not for hoarding.
On Sunday mornings bells rang.
In patent leather shoes and best clothes,
I went to church and sat on the lap of Jesus.
"Red and yellow, black and white."
We were "precious in his sight."
We fed the hungry and clothed the naked,
all for a nickel a week.
We learned to be Christian soldiers
and received stars:
gold ones just for being there,
red ones for memory work.
I forgot the memory work;
I remembered the stars . . .
and the Red Letter Testament
for a "correct recitation
of the Child's Catechism,"
a correct recitation in front of the

whole Adult Sunday School Class,
the women smelling of powder,
the men, sitting straight,
trapped in their suits.
I was six years old and already knew
that Jesus spoke in red letters.

After Sunday School, I sat in the pew
and counted the light bulbs over
the heads of the worshipers.
When I got tired, I leaned my head
on my mother's shoulder and prayed—
for church to be over.
On Tuesdays I ate cheesedreams
and smiled at the ladies who told me
I had grown since last Tuesday when
they had told me the same thing.
On Saturdays I ran in the church while
my father did whatever preachers
do in church on Saturday mornings.
On Sundays I never ran in church.

In 1942, I met the Pharisees.
They pointed their fingers at my father,
who preached Peace and Racial Equality.
They told him to stick to the Bible.
The Church stuck out its tongue,
and broke my heart.
I retreated to a tree and watched
the world careening with the stars.
I hid in that tree, high in the tree, waiting
for widows and orphans and strangers.
When they came by, I dropped

Sunday School stars in their hair,
an act of compassion, a secret mission
assigned to me by Jesus himself.
The Church in the Tree had one member . . .
just me.
There were two who knew of the
Church in the Tree . . . Jesus and me,
just Jesus and me.

The room was crowded with tall men
in dark suits.
My father stood facing me.
In gentle voice, but with great solemnity,
came the question: Who is your Lord and Savior?
The One Who Speaks in Red Letters,
He is my Lord and Savior . . . Jesus the Christ.
Jesus Christ, born under a star . . .
He is my Lord and Savior.
The Bright and Morning Star . . .
the Prince of Peace . . . the Lord of all.
This young church, this new church,
this church who believed in peace and
racial equality and in the poetry of preaching . . .
this church became my home.
I was eight years old and looking
for some good news.
I looked in my Red Letter Testament,
and there I found God's story,
a story of Sabbath and Jubilee,
a story of covenant with God
and loving your neighbors,
feeding the hungry,
clothing the naked,

and healing the sick,
a story of Jesus, born under a star,
Jesus, who brought us Life Abundant,
Jesus, who forgave those who crucified him,
Jesus, who was resurrected.
It is the story of the grace of God
falling like snow on God's people.
I listened to my father's sermons,
and there I found God's story.
I sat among the baptized,
and there I found God's story
in a church in Tennessee
where the believers tried
to live in covenant faithfulness
in justice and mercy and humility.
I grew up in their nurture;
I learned at their knee.
I quit the Church in the Tree
because it takes two or three
gathered in his name . . . in the name
of the Bright and Morning Star.
Greedily, I had hoarded my stars
until I learned love from the poor in spirit.
The story of God has everything to do
with giving away our hearts;
the stars go with them.
Presbyterian born, Presbyterian bred,
Presbyterian educated, Presbyterian wed. . . .
Granddaughter, daughter, cousin,
wife of Presbyterian clergy. . . .
Presbyterian elder. . . .
Here's the Church, and here's the steeple.
Open the door. Where are the people?

Lost sheep, lost coin, lost son, lost people.
The good shepherd looks for the lost sheep
until he finds it, and then rejoices!
Light the lamp! Sweep the house!
Search carefully until the lost coin is found.
Then call the neighbors and rejoice!
Run out and meet the lost son!
Welcome him with compassion!
Bring the best robe! And the finest ring!
Put sandals on his feet! Kill the fatted calf!
Celebrate and rejoice! He who was lost is found!
He who was dead is alive!
For we have eaten our hot cross buns
and heard the declaration of the trumpets:
He is risen! He who was dead is alive, but
we who say we believe continue our quarreling,
flipping through Bibles to find passages
to support our private theologies.
No wonder the children have left!
We forgot to teach them the story.
We taught moralisms instead of the word of God.
We've put Jesus back in the tomb,
rolled the stone back in place, and
continued to behave as though he is dead.
Have we not heard? Have we not known?
Yes, we have heard; yes, we have known,
but our hearts are hardened.
We hoard our stars and store up
treasures here on earth.
We run in church, even on Sundays.
Anxious and stressed, vying for positions and power,
we spend our energies creating more rules,
for fear of losing control.

The rules have become more important
than the freeing word of God.
We have processed the gospel into neat
little packages and stacks of paper.
We've gathered the saints into committees
and asked them to serve without starlight.
We've drained the poetry from the gospel.
We've taken the amazing out of grace
and the glory out of God.
The pew preaches to the pulpit,
and there is no poetry in it.
The way of the world sits in our
general assemblies, where we're all
decked out in clothes of righteousness.
Meanwhile, the wounded of the world still bleed,
the helpless find no help, the poor cry out in pain,
but . . . church people are quarreling. . . .
We forgot . . . we forgot . . . we forgot who we are.
What have we here that we're too afraid to say?
By the waters of Babylon the poets weep.
The lost people of God wander in the wilderness.
The sheep have scattered.
They bleat blindly, occasionally bumping
into one another in fearful frenzy . . .
lost, because we forgot . . . we forgot . . . we forgot . . .
the Way, and the Truth, and the Life.
We've wandered from worship,
and we've wandered from covenant, and
the story is told in Ho-Hum institutionalism.
The only thing we get excited about is
sex . . . and money . . . and little pieces of power.
In self-righteous indignation we spit mean-spiritedly
at those who disagree with our point of view.

We accuse falsely and point fingers at the innocent.
Wrapped in piosity, we hurt each other
in the name of Jesus.
We meet in secret and strategize.
We consult and confer with everybody but God.
It's time to stand up and be counted;
it's time to kneel down and confess. . . .
If we have the ears to hear, we will
hear the poignant whisper of God: "Return to me."
"Return to me," says the Lord.
And the Lamb of God asks:
Who do they say that I am?
Who do we say that he is?
Who do we say that he is by the way we live?
In the midst of this quarrelsome congregation,
do we mouth the words that he is
the Prince of Peace?
In this divided church do we dare to say
he is the Lord of All?
Meanwhile, our slogan has become:
Trust the process.
The trouble is we've worshiped the Process.
I learned early that the church is
fond of processing the gospel,
diluting the word of God
into more palatable portions.
Never tell a poet to trust the process.
We don't and we won't!
We'll trust the word of God,
and we'll trust the community,
but we won't trust the process.
Processing obliterates the poetry
from the lips of God.

Processing removes the danger and
risk of following the One who said
"Take up my cross. . . ."
All business and no poetry keeps
the people from tenderheartedness.
God the Poet says: "Return to me."
We forgot . . . we forgot . . . we forgot . . .
to keep covenant.
We forgot . . . we forgot . . . we forgot . . .
to keep Sabbath.
We thought we could arrive
in the Kingdom of God
without reading the instructions.
We thought God would reward us
for carrying our Bibles.
We thought we could use our Bibles
to further the gospel according to us.
The voice of God no longer whispers;
the voice of God booms:
"Is this how I want you to worship?"
No! "The worship I want is
to let the oppressed go free,
to share your bread with the hungry,
to bring the homeless into your houses,
to clothe the naked,
to stop pointing fingers and speaking evil."
Then when we call, when we cry for help,
God will answer: Here am I. . . . Here am I. . . .
Here am I in your midst.
God in our midst. . . .
So what can we do?
We can continue our quarreling,
or we can vote to the right,

or we can vote to the left,
or we can vote to the center.
If we choose to enter the center,
we must be very careful not to assume
that we are entering the Kingdom of God.
God will not be processed,
and God has never needed a majority vote.
We in the Church can vote all we want to,
but the Spirit of God will move where it will,
no matter our voting.
The gospel is still God's story,
and God the Poet says: Return to me.
God the Poet says: Keep the Sabbath.
We in the church have trampled on the Sabbath.
We've forgotten praise and thanksgiving.
We seek praise for our ideas
and thanks for all we've done.
We've forgotten our Hosannas.
We've forgotten how to say thank you.
How do we say Hosanna?
That great cloud of witnesses,
those who came before us,
those who sang their Hosannas
before we found our voice,
those are the ones who come to us.
I awoke to a bedroom full of sun and of God,
a bedroom full of Hosanna.
It's then that I see her:
She stands in the doorway with the alabaster jar,
and in a burst of Hosanna, she kneels and begins
to weep and to wash his feet with her hair,
her long and shining hair.
The Pharisee, the one who had invited

Jesus to supper, is properly shocked.
If Jesus were really a prophet,
he would know what kind of woman
this was touching him.
The woman continued her Hosanna by kissing
the feet of Jesus and tenderly anointing
them with ointment.
Oh, the house is awash in Hosannas!
Hosanna in her tears,
Hosanna in her hair,
Hosanna in each kiss,
Hosanna in the loving hands that anoint
his feet with costly ointment.
Hosanna in an alabaster jar . . .
Hosanna in the heart of a woman. . . .
Then into her Hosanna tramps Simon,
the Pharisee, but Jesus knew what
was in Simon's heart,
and Jesus told Simon a parable.
"A certain creditor had two debtors; one owed
five hundred denarii, and the other one fifty.
When they could not pay, he canceled the debts
for both of them. Now which will love him more?"
"I suppose," Simon answered, "the one for whom
he canceled the greater debt."
Jesus looks again at the Hosanna Woman,
but speaks to Simon.
The Hosanna Woman is bathed in the
light of praise, but the Pharisee is moving
to the gray shadows of faithlessness.
"Do you see this woman?" Jesus asks Simon.
Of course Simon sees her!
The woman moves in Hosannas before his eyes.

Jesus continues: "I entered your house;
you gave me no water for my feet, but she has
bathed my feet and dried them with her hair.
You gave me no kiss, but from the time I came in,
she has not stopped kissing my feet.
You did not anoint my head with oil, but
she has anointed my feet with ointment.
Therefore, I tell you, her sins, which are many,
have been forgiven; she has shown great love.
But the one to whom little is forgiven loves little."
The Hosanna Woman lives in a place
called Prayer at the feet of Jesus.
I look at the window where the
sun still shouts Hosanna!
and I look at Jesus and the Hosanna Woman,
and I say, Thank You!
How does the heart say "Thank You"?
Our mouths say what our hearts are full of. . . .
There was one who said, "Thank You!"
one out of ten . . . and Jesus asked:
"What happened to the other nine?"
Blessings on that one who taught us
how to worship!
He is the Way and the Truth and the Life,
and he walks now the dusty road to Jerusalem.
Somewhere between Samaria and Galilee,
he enters a village.
Those ten stand there, there in the village . . . ,
they stand at a distance as lepers were
required to do . . . stand at a distance,
their skin eaten with disease.
They were feared and excluded
from the normal way of living.

They stand at a distance, but
they do not keep their silence.
They call out to him:
"Jesus, Master, have mercy on us."
Jesus turns and sees them.
He calls to them to go and
show themselves to the priests.
Go to church!
They leave obeying, and as they walk along,
they are made clean.
One of them, when he sees that they are healed,
turns back, praising God in a loud voice.
The mouth says what the heart is full of. . . .
He prostrates himself at the feet of Jesus,
and says, "Thank you!"
And this man was a Samaritan!
Jesus asks him: "Were not ten made clean?
But where are they? Was none of them found to
return and give praise except this foreigner?"
Then Jesus says to the Thank-You Man:
"Get up and go your way. Your faith has made you
    well."
In a place called Prayer, I hear the leper's voice cry:
"Thank you!"
He stands in the halls of eternity,
cleansed and faithful, mouthing
the thank-you his heart is full of. . . .
I move closer, for holiness awaits
in the grateful cry of the healed.
I wait in a place called Prayer, and when
I hear the footsteps of God, I tremble.
Am I one of the nine?

Of course I'm one of the nine!
That's what the story is all about!
If I'd written the screenplay, I'd have
starred as the healed and grateful leper.
And, of course, I like to think of myself
as the Hosanna Woman!

I close the book, but the words persist:
"Listen, if you have the ears to hear!
Look, if you have the eyes to see!"
I've heard, and I've seen, and I've turned out
to be the Pharisee and one of the nine.
The thing that keeps us from
picking up that alabaster jar,
the thing that makes us
continue on our ungrateful way,
is that those of us who hang around the Church a lot
forget that the Word of God is written for us,
as well as for the others.

In the midst of our bickering and battling,
there is the persistent voice of the Holy One,
who calls even now: "Return to me."
It's time to remember who we are
and to whom we belong.
We don't have the option of the Church in the Tree,
a Church just for me, for his name is
not God-with-me,
but Emmanuel, God-with-us.
My prayer is that we will have
the eyes to see and the ears to hear
the Hosanna Woman and the Thank-You Man,

and when our hearts are sufficiently humbled,
I pray that we in his Church will forgive one another,
and stand, even at this distance, and cry to him,
"Jesus, Master, have mercy on us!"
Who do we say that he is?
Who do we say that he is by the way we live?
And how can we live with what we've been saying?

Our hot cross buns are cold,
and we've eaten the Easter candy,
but there is still time for tenderheartedness.
There's still time for compassion.
There's still time for us to be about
the business of freeing the slaves.
"Return to me," says God the Poet.
"Return to me."
There's still time for us to turn
and hand our hearts to the widows,
the orphans, and the strangers among us.
There's still time
to share our stars with
those who have no stars.
There's still time to sit down to life
with our neighbors
and share our bread and our wine.
Even now the thank-yous can rise from our hearts,
and we will no longer be concerned with
counting our number, for he is Lord of all,
and our number is still greater than
all the stars in the sky. . . .

Our mouths will sing what our hearts are full of:
Hosanna and Thank You,

and we will remember . . . remember . . . remember . . .
to love one another.
We will remember the song of the angels:
Peace on earth, goodwill to all . . .
to all . . . to all. . . .
We will live in the promise of the presence of God
when every knee . . . every knee! . . .
every knee shall bow at the name of Jesus. . . .
If we return, God will run out to meet us,
arms open to welcome us Home!

STARS FOR THE RIGHTEOUS

I heard about righteousness before I could spell it.
I heard about it in Sunday School
from a teacher who said she knew.
My mother said, No, she didn't.

We planted seeds of righteousness
in little paper cups, and put them
in the window to grow into flowers.
Just as the seeds needed sunshine and water,
we, who were children, needed righteousness rules.
If we followed the rules, we would get a star.

But poor Lynn Bryan would never get a star.
Too much, the teacher said.
Lynn had missed too much.
Even though her mother was sick,
her father could have brought her.
We can't get an attendance star
if we don't attend, now, can we?
When Sunday School was over,
I showed the rules to my brother,
who said they were dumb,
and I was dumb, too.
I started to hit him, but then I

remembered one of the rules:
Be ye kind one to another.
I didn't know whether my brother
counted as one of the anothers,
but I didn't want to take a chance.
I wanted the star.

As we headed toward the sanctuary,
I told my mother about the rules
and the star, and, even though
we were almost late for church,
she took the time to tell me that
righteousness was not about keeping rules
and not about getting stars.
Righteousness was, she said,
a gift of God for the people of faith.
Walking down the aisle, I tried to
tell her what the teacher told me,
that if I was righteous, I could go
to heaven, but she sh-h-h-d me.
I guess she did believe in
rule Number Five: Be quiet in church.

When the phone rang, my father was
coming in the door, my mother said,
"Good sermon," kissed him,
and picked up the phone.
I was trying to tell him
about the rules and the star,
when my mother sh-h-h-d me
for the second time that day, and
handed the phone to my father.
It was then that we learned
that Lynn Bryan's mother was dead.

Lynn spent the week with me, sharing
my room and my toys and my mother.
By Wednesday I knew I wouldn't get a star.
I missed choir practice because I couldn't
leave Lynn Bryan all sad and crying.
The day of the funeral, she wore her best dress
and didn't go to school.
On Saturday her father came to take her home.
I waved goodbye and turned to see my
mother standing there, her arms wide open.
I hugged her tightly and began to cry.
It's not fair, I said, Lynn Bryan would
never get a star.

I found my father behind his desk
in his study, working on his sermon.
I crawled in his red leather chair,
and asked him if he was still sad
because his Papa died when he was
just a little boy.
From time to time, he answered,
from time to time.
If I had a star, I said, I'd give it to you.
He put his paper down and looked at me.
I'm sorry about the star, he said,
about missing choir practice and all. . . .
I wouldn't have gotten it anyway, I admitted.
I can't sit still in church, not for a whole hour!

It was then my father told me the same thing
my mother had told me, that righteousness was
not about keeping a list of rules to get a star.
He said no matter how many rules I kept,
I could never earn my way into heaven.

The good news was Jesus had already paid my way.
He said that was hard for people to believe
and hard for people to remember.
My father told me that "Be ye kind" was from Jesus,
but Jesus wanted us to be kind
because we had love in our hearts,
not because we'd get a star.
Righteousness was about caring
when somebody was sad;
it was about being angry when
someone was treated unfairly.
It was about giving up your star
when the rules were not about love.

Then my father told me stories about
people that Jesus called faithful.
They weren't people who were trying
to show off about how good they were.
They were people who believed.
He even said that Jesus got mad
at some church people who thought
they were righteous, keeping rules that
had nothing to do with the love of God.
Righteousness was not about rules
written on paper, but the love of God
written on our hearts.
Righteousness had nothing to do with self
and everything to do with loving others . . .
because of our faith in Jesus.

That night I found on my pillow
a whole box of stars.
I gave one to my father, and
I gave the rest of the box to Lynn Bryan.

The funny thing was that the next night
there was another box of stars on my pillow.
It's a gift, my mother said, ·
just because I love you.
Righteousness is like that.
So is the grace of God.

GIVING UP FOR LENT

❧❧❦❦

I remember Easter egg hunts
on green lawns and in our living room.
I remember pastel dresses and patent leather shoes.
I remember roast lamb with mint jelly.
I remember the abundance of fresh flowers,
splashes of spring colors throughout the house,
and overloaded Easter baskets,
brimming with marshmallow chicks and
chocolate bunnies and foil-covered eggs.
But most of all, I remember
hot cross buns on Good Friday morning,
and going to church instead of school, and
the inevitable sermons on the last words of Jesus,
and wondering why, in the face of the cross and
     death,
this day is called "Good."
I remember trying to be still and quiet in church
and looking forward, during the last-words sermons,
to our lunch downtown.
I thought it should have been raining
and wondered if we should be having
such a good time, but my mother and father
never encouraged hypocrisy any time,
and certainly not during Lent.

Of course, at first, we didn't know it was Lent.
To those of us who were Presbyterians
down in Tennessee,
it was just the time before Easter.
My Catholic and Episcopal friends had Lent,
but we didn't.
At school one Wednesday these friends,
their foreheads marked with the morning's ash,
told about the party they had Tuesday night and
how much they ate and how late they got to stay up,
and I wished we had Lent so we could eat all that
food and candy and stay up way past our bedtime,
but that was before I heard about
"giving up" something for Lent.
It wasn't long before they were
asking me what I had given up.
Of course, I didn't know what
they were talking about.

When they told me they couldn't
eat chocolate or ice cream or cake or
whatever they had "given up," I was horrified.
They gave up eating something wonderful
until Easter morning.
What on earth would they do that for?
I felt more than a little stupid
when they told me I had to
"give up" something for Lent
because my father was a priest.
I told them, no, my father was not a priest!
He was a minister, and they said,
well, same thing, so I had to
"give up" chocolate or something.

My mother said, no, I didn't
have to "give up" a thing.
She said that Jesus had already
"given up" his life for us,
and that was enough . . . for all time.
The very next day I told my friends
that I didn't have to "give up" anything,
and they asked me how I was going
to remember Jesus.
I didn't get it; I told them
I hadn't forgotten Jesus!
They laughed, and said that
they remember Jesus, every time
they don't eat chocolate or
whatever it was they gave up for Lent.
My mother said that we remember Jesus
all the time, not just during Lent,
and if my friends want to
"give up" something for Lent,
they shouldn't talk about it all the time.
They should just quietly not eat
what they had "given up," and
take their sacrifice seriously.
I thought they were taking it seriously.
After all, they talked about it every day,
talked about how hard it was
to do without chocolate,
talked about the solid chocolate bunnies
they would get in their Easter baskets.
They hinted that I might be in danger of
hellfire if I didn't "give up" something,
but my mother seemed perfectly happy
with our status as far as heaven

was concerned, or so she said.
When I really got worried was when
one of my friends at school told me
her father said that "giving up"
something for Lent was in the Bible.
My mother told me to get my
Red Letter Testament and read Matthew,
the sixth chapter, especially the
sixteenth through the eighteenth verses.
I did, and it turned out to be
about being a hypocrite if you fast
and brag about it all the time.
Then I read what my friend's father
told her to read, from Joel 2:12.
Horrors! I ran to my mother and
told her that God wants us to fast
after all, and all this time
I didn't fast while my friends did.
Did that mean I had to stay
in hell for a longer time than they had to?
My mother looked at me as though
she didn't recognize me, and asked me to
read aloud to her the Joel passage.
"Yet even now, says the Lord,
return to me with all your heart,
with FASTING" (I read "fasting" in
a very loud I-told-you-so voice),
"with weeping, and with mourning;
rend your hearts and not your clothing."
That's it, my mother said.
"Rend your hearts and not your clothing!"
Sometimes I just did not know
what my mother was talking about.

She tried to explain that
I could fast if I wanted to,
but that it should be a private matter,
something between me and God,
an act of worship, an act of prayer.
She said I shouldn't show off
like the Pharisees who told
everybody about their fasting.
Instead I should examine my heart.
I looked up "rend" in the dictionary
and found out it meant "tear."
Tear your heart instead of your clothes!
That didn't make sense to me!
I thought maybe I should check
with my father, but he was pretty busy
with all those extra services of worship.

On Good Friday we didn't have to get up early
because we didn't have to go to school.
We began the day with a big breakfast,
heavy on the hot cross buns.
Then we played until it was time
to get dressed and go to church.
We drove to a downtown church,
where our father was preaching
one of those last-words sermons.
I wasn't really listening all that much
until I heard him say:
"Return to me with all your heart,
with fasting, with weeping, and with mourning;
rend your hearts and not your clothing."
I elbowed my brother who was sitting next
to me and told him to elbow our mother.

He did, and she looked at me and nodded.
Yes, she'd heard the words, too.
She smiled at me, and looked back at my father.
who began his sermon by asking:
"What does God mean by that?"
I jabbed my brother so that he could
get my mother's attention.
He made a face and told me to Sh-h-h!
but my mother saw us and
nodded to me and smiled again.
The answer to that question is
just what I wanted to know, too!
When the sermon was over,
I couldn't remember a lot of it,
but what I've never forgotten is this:
God asks us for a fasting of the heart,
a "giving up" of whatever it is that
keeps us from loving one another,
a "giving up" of whatever it is that
keeps us living our own stories
instead of living God's story.
My father read from Isaiah 58 where it says
that the kind of fasting God wants is this:
to work for justice,
to help the oppressed,
to share our bread with the hungry,
to give clothes to those who have no clothes,
and to help our relatives.
That didn't sound like fasting to me, but
my father went on to say that a fasting
of the heart meant that our hearts ached
when somebody was treated unfairly,
that the ache was so bad that

we had to do something about it,
just like we'd want somebody else to do
if we were the ones being treated unfairly.
My father said that Jesus preached about
the oppressed people living in his time
and quoted this very scripture from Isaiah.
Then my father said there are also
oppressed people living in our time.
These are the ones we need to free.
Then he listed some people living in Nashville
that were oppressed and treated unfairly.
These people were treated unfairly
because of the color of their skin,
or the observances of their faith,
or the accents in their voices,
or their poverty,
or even because they wanted peace.
The greatest fast, he said,
would be to help them.
If the Christian churches wouldn't help,
who would?
I knew even then that there was a lot
I didn't understand about all this, but
I was beginning to see a little more clearly.
Fasting has little to do with what
I "give up" unless the "giving up"
helps me to remember that
so many have so little, and
the remembering moves me to
share my bread as well as my heart.
My father said that a fasting of the heart
meant "giving up" some of our selfishness.
He said that everybody is selfish, but

as followers of Jesus, we can begin
to learn how to be less selfish.
We can allow our hearts
to ache for somebody else.
When I first learned about the
fasting of the heart, it was Good Friday.
I thought perhaps I didn't deserve
to celebrate on Easter Day.
After church we went to the B&W Cafeteria
and had to stand in line for some time.
I asked my father why he didn't preach
that sermon before Good Friday.
"I did," he said. "You just didn't hear it."
My little sister said that she heard it,
but I knew she didn't because she was
trying to think of what dessert
she was going to order while
I was thinking of giving up
my usual order of baked custard.
I didn't know whether it would make me
remember to share my bread or not,
and I didn't know how to find poor people
to give the bread to anyway,
when my brother told me it was too late.
By this time we had begun our way
down the cafeteria line, and
my brother had just plopped a big piece
of chocolate cake down on his tray.
"Too late for you!" my brother said.
"Fatty!" I called him.
He said, "Skeleton!" back to me.
The verbal warfare was escalating
when my father stopped it by saying

that "giving up" calling my brother
"Fatty" would be a good idea.
When he said that I got all red in the face
and felt I would burn in hell for sure.
I said I was sorry, first to the air,
and then to my brother.
He mumbled something to me that
I wasn't sure was an apology,
but I let it go because I was at
the place in the cafeteria line
where I had to make a decision
about the baked custard.
"Take it," my mother said.
"You've given up enough for one day."
I hesitated because I knew she didn't
believe in giving up food for Lent.
I hesitated for a few seconds,
but then I took the baked custard.
At the end of the meal I said,
"Guess what? I still remember Jesus."
In the afternoon my father said he was going
calling on some sick people in the church.
Would anybody want to go with him?
Everybody else said no, but I said, yes,
hoping that this act of kindness would
help me on the path to heaven.
Our first stop was the hospital.
I stayed in the waiting room
while my father asked the woman
if she was up to having another visitor.
He asked that because she had fallen
and broken her legs when she had
learned of the death of her son

who was a pilot in the war.
I knew this woman, and I liked her a lot,
and I felt terrible about her son.
In just a minute my father was back.
"She'd like to see you," he said.
We went in and she smiled at me,
and thanked me for coming to see her.
I told her I was so sorry she had
broken her legs, and I was so sorry
her son had died in the war.
She held her hand out, and I held it
the whole time we were there,
and she got tears in her eyes
when my father said we had to leave,
and he said a prayer,
and when I opened my eyes,
she had more tears in her eyes,
but she smiled, and said
I would never know what it meant
to her that I came to visit, and
I hugged her and we all said,
good-bye.
When we got in the car, my father said
that he was very proud of me.
I said that I didn't know why,
because I didn't "give up" anything.
He said, no, you didn't give up anything,
at least not something like chocolate,
but you "gave up" thinking about yourself,
and you thought about somebody else,
about somebody else's pain.
You saw not only the pain
from her broken legs,

but you saw the pain
from her broken heart.
You may not have fasted as
your friends have fasted, but
your heart gave up thinking about
how you were going to get to heaven,
and instead you visited someone
who needed you very much.
I hated to disappoint my father, but
I thought I ought to tell him right away
that the reason I went visiting was that
I hoped it would help me get to heaven.
I hoped that in some way it would
make up for not fasting.
I know that, he said, I know that,
but your heart took over once you
saw her lying there, needing you.
Sometimes I didn't understand my father
any better than I understood my mother.
I knew that it was my father
who was needed at this time.
I guess it was nice to take a little girl along,
but it was my father's presence that counted
that day in the hospital down in Tennessee.
Besides, I said, I didn't do anything
to work for justice
or help the oppressed
or share my bread with the hungry
or give clothes to those who don't have any clothes
and I know, for sure, I didn't help our relatives.
He laughed and said I was so literal.
I knew literary meant something about
reading a lot, but I didn't know what

that had to do with fasting.
Maybe he meant I needed to read more
about fasting or read the Bible more often.
Whatever it was, I was still uneasy.

On Easter morning our baskets were
as full as could be, and we were even
allowed to eat a little candy before church.
After breakfast we went to the sunrise
service and then to the first service,
and then we went home.
Of course, my father didn't come home
until almost one o'clock.
My mother wanted to
get a head start on dinner.
We had a lamb roast with mint jelly
and green beans and yellow squash
with cracker crumbs and butter
and mashed potatoes and gravy and
cherry jello with walnuts and cream cheese
and Gladys's homemade rolls and
for dessert we had angel food cake
with boiled custard, my favorite.
After dinner, I asked my mother if
we could take a plate of Easter dinner
to the woman I saw in the hospital
because the food there probably
wasn't very good, at least not
good enough for Easter dinner.
I'm not trying to get to heaven, I said.
I just thought it might be nice.
It would be nice, my mother said,
and I know you're not trying to do

"good works" to get to heaven.
Isn't it great that heaven is a gift of God?
She began to prepare a plate.
Heaven is a gift of God,
I repeated to myself.
Heaven is a gift of God. . . .
My mother and I went to deliver
the Easter dinner even though
she had declared earlier that
she would never go calling on
Easter or on Christmas.
The rest of the day was spent in celebration.
As the day went by our Easter baskets
dwindled considerably.
We all knew that Easter was
not about the Easter Bunny,
although we enjoyed our Easter baskets,
nor was it about new clothes,
although we had them,
nor was it about eating,
although we surely had an abundance.
Easter is a celebration that Jesus is alive,
a celebration that nothing, not even Death,
can separate us from the love of God.
What I learned that particular Lenten season
is that whether or not we fast,
heaven is a gift of God.

WAR AND HATE

꧁꧂

When the War came, hate came, too.
It sat on our doorsteps and came into
our living rooms and sang its
seductive songs from our radios.
The newsreels at the movies
filled our heads with certain
images of the enemy:
German soldiers with their
high-step marching,
and later the Japanese in their
fast-flying suicide planes,
and Mussolini, who seemed to spend
the war waving from his balcony.
Enemy faces, evil and monstrous, watched
us from billboards along the highways
and posters on the sides of buildings.
On the playground we played "Nazi,"
with goose step and stiff-armed
Heil Hitlers just like in the newsreel.
The boys were especially fond
of playing the kamikaze pilots.
With arms straight out and
irritatingly loud plane noises
emerging from their throats,

they would run smack into a
group of girls and commence
to "explode" in their midst.
We all knew how wicked and
horrible our enemies were,
while the Allies, led by the ever
strong Americans, were the good
guys, courageous and true.
You can imagine my surprise, then,
when our parents asked us
to consider not singing the very
catchy and popular patriotic war tune:
"Praise the Lord, and Pass the Ammunition."
My father said,
"Think about the words you sing."
It had never occurred to me that
war was a theological matter.
I had forgotten how upset some of
the people were when my father
preached the sermon on peace
just before the Second World War.
I thought our whole family was
as patriotic as could be.

My father stood in the doorway,
extra gas ration coupons in his hand,
the green booklets flapping in the
October breeze, as he explained
to us again, before he drove away,
that he would never use the extra
coupons except to call on the sick
or to drive to conduct a funeral.
The joyriding had stopped long ago.

Sunday-afternoon calling was a
thing of the past unless it was
to visit the sick or dying.
Of course, there were rumors of
clergymen, as well as doctors,
who used the extra gas rations
for their own pleasure driving.
Certainly not our father, who
very meticulously recorded
every mile he drove!
I knew he was going now on a
car trip he didn't want to make.
He was going now to comfort
a family whose son and brother
had gone to war and was never
ever coming home.
There were far too many of
those visits to suit my father . . .
far too many, he'd say.
Then he'd pick up the gas rations
and say, I wish the coupons *could*
be used on pleasure.
Sometimes I would hear the phone
ring in the middle of the night,
and could hear my father call
to my mother: Missing in action.
Then he would call out a name,
and stirring sounds would begin.
As I heard the water splashing,
the kettle whistling, the door closing,
and the car's engine starting,
I would repeat the name over
and over and over into the

silent darkness of my room.
One night in the haziness of sleep,
I overheard my mother and father
talking and suddenly realized that
they were talking about my father
enlisting in the war.
He said he felt that he was not
making the same sacrifice that
the other men were making . . .
the men who went away to war.
My mother said that she wanted
to be brave, but that my father
could hardly expect her to be brave
when it came to losing him.
That made us think our father
was going away to war, and
we would never see him again.
I began to say my prayers two
times each night and begged God
not to let my Daddy go to war.
Sometimes I cried, from the fear of it.
My father said that Mr. Roosevelt said
there's nothing to fear, but fear itself.
I said, oh, yes, there is, Mr. Roosevelt!
There was the fear that my Daddy
might go off to war.
My father decided to see the Navy Man
in charge of chaplains.
This Navy Man asked my father
how he felt about going off to war.
My father said he didn't believe war
would ever solve the problems of
the world, but he felt he should

take the same risk and responsibility
that the men in his church took.
He said he wasn't afraid to go to war,
but he couldn't kill anybody and he
certainly couldn't hate the enemy.
He wanted to do his part to help
the men who had gone to war,
the ones who might need him
when they were scared or dying.
He said he'd hoped that he might
make a good chaplain to the men
who would be facing war and death.
The Navy Man looked him right
in the eye and asked him if he
realized he, too, would be facing death.
My father said it wasn't death he was
afraid of . . . it was not doing the right thing,
not being faithful.
After they talked, the Navy Man told
my father that he thought the best
thing my father could do for the
men who went to war was to stay
home and care for their families,
that these men were counting on
my father to comfort their families
while they were away.
The Navy Man told him that sometimes
the hardest thing was to stay home.
Even so, my father decided to take
the medical test just in case the
Navy might need him in a hurry.
When he came home, he told us
that the Navy told him he

couldn't see well enough to hit
the side of a barn and so
he couldn't join the Navy,
but thank you anyway.
I knew my father felt bad,
afraid he wasn't doing his part,
afraid he wasn't doing the right thing,
afraid he wasn't being faithful,
so we tried to cheer him up when
we told him that all the ladies and
the children and the older men who
couldn't go to war were happy that
my father would be there with us.
So my father stayed home and
the other men went away to war.
Over and over and over again these
men told my father, "Thank you."
So, my father was doing his part
for the war effort even though
he thought he wasn't doing
as much as the other men.
My mother had a victory garden,
full of onions and radishes and
green beans, and she was proud to
tell us she was doing her part, too.
She even got a job for the war effort.
She would get up early and take a bus
to the Vultee plant and was a
manager until we got out of school.
Then she would rush home and
make us an afterschool snack.
She said there were some people
in the congregation who gossiped

about her because the minister's wife
wasn't supposed to have a job.
She said the church didn't pay
my father enough money and
accused him of being unpatriotic,
but criticized her when she went
to work to help make ends meet
and help with the war effort, too.
She said she didn't have time
for gossipers, and went right on
gardening and working at Vultee
and organizing women at the USO
to make and take refreshments
for the soldiers stationed nearby,
the soldiers who didn't have
any home cooking.
Sometimes the make-and-take
women couldn't make and take,
so we would make cookies, and
take them to the USO and
for a very short time while
we waited for our mother,
we were allowed to watch
the soldiers and the girls
from Nashville dance at the USO.
Each Sunday Gladys invited soldiers
who attended our church services to
come home and have dinner with us.
My father said he was amazed that
my mother could manage to feed
so many so often with so small
a piece of meat.
We called her the casserole queen,

but vowed we'd never eat tuna
again when the war was over.
Of course, our mother could even
make Spam taste good . . . sort of.
She said it was the flavor of the
onions and garlic that she grew
in her victory garden.
Besides, she said, garlic is good
for what ails you.

We were patriotic children, too.
We took the labels off each tin can,
removed the bottom of the can,
as well as the top, so that
we could flatten the cans and the
tin could be used in the war effort.
My brother even learned how to knit,
and knitted an orange sweater to keep
someone warm, someone in the war.
My mother was terribly proud of him
for this, and I could imagine some
poor soul far, far away overseas,
right in the middle of the war,
bombs exploding around him,
no food, no place to hide,
but in the midst of all of this,
he was warm because he was
wearing a bright orange sweater
that my brother had knitted.

Besides all of this, my mother would
save as much of our sugar supply
as possible for Christmas baking
and then send a cake to our relatives

in England and in Scotland.
We tried to save some of our rations
and send them a tin of ham, too,
" . . . if at all possible," my mother would say.
We wrapped and labeled small
and light presents and wrapped
the ham and the cake in
festive paper we had colored
with our crayons, and then
we tied the packages with bits
of bright orange wool left over
from the sweater effort.
We put them all in boxes
just the right sizes and took
the boxes to the post office.
The packages had to be sent
months before Christmas,
and we didn't hear about the
successful arrival of the boxes
sometimes for another four
or even five months.
The day we mailed the boxes
was a day of victory for our war effort!
We knew we were all patriotic,
but some of those people
who had criticized my father,
because he preached Peace, said
he was a sissy and a communist.
My father said just ignore them;
they didn't know what they were
talking about.

Every night we said our prayers
and prayed that the people in

our church who had gone to war
would be safe.
My father said what about the
people in other churches and
what about the people
who didn't go to church.
I didn't know there were people
who didn't go to church,
and I thought that everybody
prayed every night for
their own people whether
there was war or not.
My father said that Jesus
prayed for everybody, so
I added "all the people from
the United States who
are fighting in the war."
My prayers were getting
very long, and I thought
surely there was nothing
else I had to include, when
my father said: "What about
the German children whose
daddies are fighting in the war?"
"That's the enemy," I answered.
"German children?" he asked.
I wondered if my father knew
that the children at our school
called the enemy very bad names.
Then my mother came in, and
I was glad because I was very
confused about the war and the
enemies and Jesus,

and people I should hate,
and people I should love.
She said that right now there
were little German children
saying their prayers to God, asking
God to keep their daddies safe.
I had no idea that the enemy prayed.
Just like me. . . . "People are alike
all over the world," my mother said.
"They don't want war either. It's some
of the leaders who start the wars."
She said she thought someday
we would just send all the people
who liked to fight, to a big island
out in the middle of the ocean,
and then the rest of us would
stay home in peace.
So I added to my prayers
"all the children of the
whole wide world."
It was not long after this that
it occurred to me that I should
also add their daddies and
mommies and everybody
who wanted to live in peace.
My father heard my struggle
and said that Jesus told us
to pray for our enemies.
I knew he was going to say that!
In my heart I knew that my Daddy
wanted me to pray for our enemies,
but I had visions of evil soldiers
(the enemy), and visions

of good soldiers (the Allies),
and I thought it would be
unpatriotic for sure to pray
for the enemy.
I looked at my father and
he looked pretty sure about
what Jesus had said, and
if Jesus told us to pray for
our enemies, I guess I would.
I just didn't tell my friends.
Well, I did tell Martha, but
I could tell her anything.
My father always seemed
to have different ideas from
the fathers of my friends, but
no matter what my father said,
Martha said what a good man
my father was, and he must
be right because he knows
about God and Jesus.
I agreed. He must be right.
But every time Martha and I
went to the Happiness Club
at the Belle Meade Theatre
on a Saturday afternoon,
I saw that poster of Uncle Sam
with his finger pointing at me,
and he was saying to me:
I WANT YOU!
Martha said that was just to
get men to join the Army,
but I wondered if it was
because I was not as patriotic

as I thought I was.
Maybe Uncle Sam wanted me
because I prayed for the enemy.
Then Martha said she thought
Jesus was much more important
than Uncle Sam.
That's funny, because that's
exactly what my mother said.
I wondered if my mother had
talked to Martha, but Martha said,
no, she just thought it up by herself.
I told my father that Martha said he
was right about praying for the enemy.
My father said Jesus was the one
who said to pray for your enemies.
Later Martha and I decided we'd
just pray for "everybody in the
whole wide world."
The only trouble with that was
it would shorten my prayers, and
my mother would turn out the light
a lot sooner, and I'd have to go to
sleep too early to suit me.
My brother said Martha and I
ought to knit sweaters
for the boys overseas.
I suspected he still had some
bright orange wool somewhere.
I don't know why he thought that
would solve my prayer problems.
Maybe he thought while Martha and
I were talking about our prayers,
we might as well be doing something

for the war effort.
Actually I think maybe Martha
did knit, but I didn't.
One night before we went to bed,
Gladys read a story called
"The First Christmas Tree."
Of all things, the first Christmas
tree was guess where? Germany!
I was skeptical until my brother
told me it was true.
He knew all sorts of things
nobody else ever knew.
Even some of the teachers at
school would ask my brother
about things they didn't know.
When I started thinking about
the German daddies and mommies
and little children decorating the
Christmas trees to celebrate the
birth of Jesus, I knew for sure
that our enemy loved Jesus.
If we loved Jesus and the enemy
loved Jesus, why were we
killing each other?
My father said now I knew why
he couldn't hate the enemy.
From then on, I thought of
our enemies as people just
like we were, sending their
daddies and their brothers
off to war and decorating their
Christmas trees and wondering
if they should include the enemy

when they said their prayers
and got tucked in at night.
The enemy was just like we were,
trapped in a war none of us wanted,
because some men, a few men in some
of the countries, wanted war.
But why would they want war?
My mother said it always came
back to this: Power and Money.
My father said it was the same way
in the Church . . . not just one church,
but the big old Church: Power and Money.
I couldn't believe my father said that!
How could that be, I asked him,
if Jesus tells us "to love one another"?
"A little child shall lead them,"
my mother said and smiled.
She was always saying that when
we said something she really liked,
but I didn't know why she liked what
I said when everybody knew that
Jesus said "love one another."
Everybody knows it, my father said,
but doing it is another thing,
even in the "big old Church."
I wondered what hope there was
for the world if people in the
Church didn't love one another.
My mother said it was very hard
for her to love the people who
hated my father, but that she
prayed that God would give her
the strength to try.

Well, I said, I don't love the
people who are mean to us,
remembering that only last Sunday
my brother and I had talked about
how much we hated one of the women
in the Church who had been very
mean to my brother.
The only reason she had been mean
to him was because she hated my
father because he preached
about loving other people who
were not like ourselves.
We had to love her?
Jesus says, Love your enemies,
my mother repeated.
Uh-oh, this was much more
complicated than I had realized.
I didn't love that woman one bit!
In fact, my brother and I had seen her
coming down the hall last Sunday
and we ran the opposite way,
my brother saying, "Hurry!
She's going to get you!"
I was laughing and scared all at once
until we ducked into the elevator and
hid until someone on the second floor
finally pushed the button.
I was still giggling when the door opened
and we got out upstairs, undiscovered.
It was so much fun.
Uh-oh, I realized how much fun it
was for my brother and me to hate
that mean old woman!

My father said we especially had
to love the people we had the
most trouble loving.
The hardest thing, he said, was to forgive
someone who didn't ask for forgiveness,
but if we don't, the hate in our hearts
festers like a boil.
It all sounded hopelessly horrible
to me, the only happy thought being
that my brother was guilty, too.
I couldn't see him giving up his
hatred of that woman after
she was so mean to him.
What if we still hate somebody?
I asked my father.
Well, he said:
Throw yourself on the grace of God.
Then he laughed, and said somebody
had told him that when he was just
a little boy.
He said the cook at his house was
named Aunt Harriet.
We'd already heard Aunt Harriet stories,
and hoped this wasn't the one about the
time he was eleven years old and
wanted to be a missionary and
Aunt Harriet brought all her grandsons
to hear my father preach out in the barn.
Aunt Harriet, he said, that smile still
big on his face, cooked everybody's
breakfast to order whenever they
came downstairs in the morning.
My father was delighted with

this system and often talked to
Aunt Harriet as he ate his breakfast.
She was a woman of deep faith and
shared her faith with everyone she knew.
One morning she told my father that
she was ashamed of him and his
brothers for picking on their cousin.
My father stopped the story long enough
to say that this cousin was the kind
of boy that was easy to upset, and
my father and his brothers had teased
him unmercifully for a very long time.
When Aunt Harriet fussed at my father,
he felt terrible, but instead of repenting,
he lashed out at Aunt Harriet and,
over a plateful of delicious hot cakes she
had made especially the way he liked them,
he said: "I hate you!"
I didn't know my father had ever hated anyone.
He said, "Of course, I didn't hate her;
it was because I loved her so much
that I felt so ashamed.
When a boy knows he's done wrong,
he usually blames somebody else."
What did she do, we asked.
"She looked me right in the eye,
and said, 'You can hate me all
you want to, but that's not going
to stop me from loving you.'"
He said he just ran out the door,
leaving his hot cakes swimming
in the butter that Aunt Harriet had
churned and the hot maple syrup

she had boiled that very morning.
Later his mother made him say he
was sorry to Aunt Harriet, but she said,
"No reason to apologize to me;
you better apologize to your cousin
and throw yourself on the grace of God."
Why'd she say that? we wanted to know.
"Because she knew what I had to learn:
Only God can forgive the meanness in us.
We stopped teasing our cousin,
and Aunt Harriet kept on cooking
our special orders and kept on loving us,
no matter what . . . kind of like the grace of God . . . ,"
he said, his voice trailing off into silence,
and I knew he was thinking about the
good old days growing up in South Carolina
and learning about Jesus from Aunt Harriet.
That night I had to ask God to forgive
me for hating the woman who was so
mean to my brother, but I didn't really
start loving her.
After all, she wasn't at all like Aunt Harriet.
She wasn't even like the little German
children who missed their daddies
and decorated the Christmas trees
and loved Jesus.
She was more like our enemy.
The next Sunday during the Bible Quiz,
I jumped up and gave the right answer.
The Mean Lady said no, that was wrong,
and told me to sit down.
A boy sitting in front jumped up and
gave the same answer,

and she said, "Right, Bobby. Very good."
The people sitting around me started
looking at me and saying,
That's what you said!
Afterwards one of the other teachers told
the Mean Lady that I had been correct.
I went home and told my mother and father
that the Mean Lady hated me, too.
My brother said she was probably a spy,
and my father said, now, now,
but our mother rolled her eyes.
I wondered if she was having
difficulty loving the Mean Lady, too.
At prayer meeting on Wednesday night,
the Mean Lady came toward me and before
I could get away, she grabbed my arm
and said that she was so sorry about
not hearing my answer correctly
and would I please forgive her.
I said, yes, and then she told me
she was getting a hearing aid and
felt so bad about all the mistakes
she had been making lately.
Then she said she had never known
two children who were so good at
the Bible Quiz as my brother and I,
and then she said she hoped I would
like the chocolate cake she had baked
for tonight's refreshments.
She said the cake was a favorite of
her grandson's who had gone off to war.
When I told my brother what she had said,
he said maybe she wasn't so bad after all

and probably wasn't a spy either.
So we forgave her because she asked us to
and made really good chocolate cake.
We even felt sorry for her because we
thought she was scared and sad
about her grandson being in the war.
My father said some people can't be very
nice when they're upset about something.
It doesn't excuse them, he said,
but it does explain them.
When I thought about the Mean Lady,
I felt sorry for her because she
probably never had an Aunt Harriet or a
father who could tell about Aunt Harriet.
If she had, she could have thrown herself
on the grace of God.
I asked my father, if I threw myself
on the grace of God, would God forgive
the meanness in me.
He looked at me, and I thought he
had a little tiny smile on his lips
when he said, "I didn't know
you had any meanness in you."
Yes, I did, I said, and told him how
much my brother and I had hated
the Mean Lady, but now she had
said she was sorry and her grandson
was in the war, and she's deaf,
and we had forgiven her, and she
makes really good chocolate cake,
and will God forgive us?
No doubt about it, my father said.
No doubt about it.

Except there was a doubt,
and my brother thought about it:
We didn't like the Mean Lady
until she asked us to forgive her.
We didn't love our enemy. . . .
Our father said that we were
learning about love and hate
and what Jesus came to tell
the world, and he thought we
were doing a good job of it.
Of course, our father and our
mother always seemed to think
we were doing a good job
at whatever we were working on.
Looking back, I had no idea that
today we'd still be working on
the same thing.

I never knitted an orange sweater to
keep somebody warm during the war,
but I did learn so many years ago
that war never solved anything
in the world or in the Church,
that Jesus said, Love your enemies,
that hate festers in your heart until
it boils over and devours your soul,
that when you feel yourself
overcome with hatred, it's time
to throw yourself on the grace of God.

SAVING GRACE

Ever since my memory first started working,
I've known that my brother saved me.
I've been told enough times!
When I was not quite two, and we lived
on Hillsboro Road in the big house
when my father was a minister downtown
in Nashville, I climbed over the railing
on the second floor, and since there was
nothing on the other side, I began to fall.
The story goes that my mother was bringing
in the groceries, and my brother looked up
and saw me falling and held out his arms.
He caught me, and I suppose, but nobody
remembers, that he fell as he caught me,
but he did catch me, and neither of us
was hurt at all.
He saved me, and the story
has never been forgotten.

Nor was the time when I was two,
and we were making a long cross-
country train trip to California,
and I climbed all over the backs
of the seats, and the train lurched

and I went flying through the air
and landed in the lap of one
very surprised gentleman.
That lovely man saved your life,
my mother told me.
There was also the time when
my mother was again bringing
in the groceries.
I was still two years old and saw
a beautiful bunch of bananas in the bag,
nine large and delicious bananas.
I took them and hid under the porch
and ate every one of the bananas.
My mother said that I must have
heard her calling, and my brother
calling, and then my father calling,
but I didn't answer until I had finished
every delicious banana.
When I was finally discovered by my
now hysterical mother, she called
the doctor who hurried over,
thinking I would certainly need to
go to the hospital and have my
stomach pumped, but I was all right.
That doctor saved your life,
my mother said.

It was Christmas 1940, when we
expected the baby to come,
right on the 25th, just like Jesus.
But the baby didn't come on
Christmas Day.
He didn't come on New Year's Day either.

My sister and I thought that
the baby had decided not to
come to our house after all.
My mother said the baby was
too coming!
Way back at Halloween time
I came home from a party and
I was very happy because we had
bobbed for apples, and I had won!
When I saw my mother waiting
for me on the porch, I ran and jumped
in her arms and then she screamed,
and I didn't know what had happened,
but the doctor said the baby was breech.
My mother was not mad at me, but she
said when I jumped in her arms,
the baby did a flip-flop, so she went
to the doctor who turned the baby
back around. I was happy.
Then the next thing I knew was
that the baby had flip-flopped again.
The doctor said that my jump
into my mother's arms had nothing
to do with the turning after all.
I wasn't so sure.
Anyway, the baby wouldn't come.
From time to time somebody would
say to me or to my sister, Jane,
"That stork sure is taking his time!"
They would laugh, but we thought
it was dumb because we knew that
babies weren't delivered by storks.
We had promised that we wouldn't

tell other little children where
the babies came from because their
parents told them the stork story.
From the 25th on, our father would
wake us and say: "The baby came!"
My sister and I would run downstairs
and there was our mother, big as life,
the baby still in her tummy.
She would laugh and so would
our father, but we didn't think
it was so funny.
So we stopped believing him and
didn't run downstairs anymore
in the mornings when he woke us,
telling us the baby was here.
So when one morning he woke us
and told us the baby had come,
we didn't move and then he said,
"You have a little baby brother."
Then we began to jump up and
down on the beds, which we weren't
allowed to do and only did after
our mother and father tucked us in
and left the room.
On this morning, the morning of
the new baby, we jumped up
and down and didn't even care
if our Daddy saw us, which he did.
He was so happy that he didn't
make us stop, and my sister
and I bounced and bounced
until we were exhausted and
then our father said, "Get dressed

and I'll take you to see your mother
and your new baby brother."

When the baby was learning to walk,
I hoped he would climb on something
so I could save him when he fell,
and then, for the rest of his life,
everybody would tell him that
I had saved him.
He climbed, but he didn't climb
over a second-floor balcony, so
I didn't get to save him that way.
When the baby was two and got mad
when we called him the baby,
we went to eat at a restaurant
in Ocean Grove, New Jersey,
far far away from Tennessee.
The bad thing was that we had to
stand in line for a very long time.
Everybody came straight from
church to this restaurant.
My mother said the long line
showed what good food they
had at this restaurant,
mainly fish which we all liked.
When we finally got to the front
of the line, the lady seating us
said we could be seated sooner
if we would divide up and
sit at three separate tables.
My mother liked it because she
got to sit with Daddy, but
Tommy had to sit with Jane,

and I had to sit with Bill.
I didn't mind except I knew I
would probably be embarrassed
because his voice was so loud.
My mother said never mind . . .
just be careful to take the
bones out of his fish.
When the dinner came, and
I had gotten all the bones
out of his fish, I started taking
the bones out of mine.
Suddenly, Bill started choking
and coughing up a storm.
His face got all red, and he
was sputtering to beat the band.
I got up and rushed over to
his side of the table and
hit him hard on the back,
and yelled for help from
my mother, and grabbed a piece
of bread and told him to eat it
to push the bone down.
Our mother had told us to do that.
He stuffed the roll in his mouth
and before my mother could get
to our table, he was better.
My mother said I had saved him,
and the people at the tables
around us said I was wonderful
and he was brave.
I had saved the baby, and now
I could tell him when he got a
memory that I had saved him

and he would probably do the
dishes for me when he got old
enough to do them.
I told Tommy that now that
I had saved somebody I
didn't have to do the dishes
for him anymore, but he said
it didn't work that way.
I still owed him everything
because he had saved my life.
I said, well, I had saved
Bill's life, and he said one thing
had nothing to do with another.
Later, I heard my mother telling
my aunt, that, by the grace of God,
that bone didn't stay stuck in
Bill's throat.
I said it wasn't God; it was me,
and she said, God needed you,
that's for sure! and she was so
proud of me that she thought
we'd have fudge that very night,
wouldn't that be fun?
We had fudge, but nobody said
how great it was that I had saved
the baby except if I mentioned it.
I told Tommy that I wouldn't
do what he said anymore because
he didn't save me, God did,
but he always had some answer
that confused me.
He said he was the instrument
of God, and as such, I owed him.

Well, then Bill owes me, I said.
He's just a baby, he said.
You should have saved Jane.
I knew I couldn't have saved Jane
because she was only a year and
eight months younger than I was,
and I thought she'd probably be
able to save herself.
After all, when we went to the zoo
in New York, she wasn't afraid to
ride on that big elephant, but I was.
She rode on it the first time around,
and I didn't ride on it until the third
when Tommy said if I didn't get on it,
I was a sissy.
So I rode the elephant, but I knew Jane
was an unlikely candidate to be saved.
Tommy never saved her either so he
must have thought the same thing.
One day in church, my father said
that we couldn't save ourselves;
that it was only by the grace of God
that we could be saved.
At lunch my mother was talking
to my father about the sermon
as she often did each Sunday.
If a person can't save herself,
I said, can she save somebody else?
I asked because the Sunday School
Teacher had told us about the
missionaries who had gone
to other countries to save the people
who had never heard of Jesus.

My mother didn't give my father
a chance to answer.
You can't save yourself and you
can't save anybody else, she said.
We are all saved by the grace of God.
Tommy said I should have known that
from learning the Child's Catechism.
I could really memorize easily,
but I didn't always know what
it was I was saying.
My father said didn't I know
that we were already saved,
and I said I wasn't talking
about that kind of saving.
I was talking about when Tommy
saved my life and I saved Bill's life.
Jane said nobody had saved her life,
but she thought maybe she had
been more careful than I had been
because she didn't climb all around
over train seats and all.
My father said we were talking
about saving bodies and he was
talking about saving souls.
My brother asked if you saved
somebody's body, didn't you save
their soul, too, but that if you
saved their soul, you didn't
necessarily save their body.
Not long afterwards, my brother
saved my life for the second time.
He and our cousin had run away
from me, and I had followed them

down a country road and onto the
railroad track. He discovered me
when we all saw the train coming.
The trouble was we were walking
on the tracks over the highway and
there was no place to hide.
Tommy grabbed me and told
me to lie down on the bank
beside the railroad track
over the highway.
I did and Tommy did and
our cousin did and we heard
the loudest noise we'd ever
heard as the train passed
just inches from us.
Tommy was so happy that we
didn't die that he wasn't even
mad at me for following them.
He just made me promise not
to tell anyone. I agreed, and I
thanked him for saving me again.
That night when I was lying in
my bed, looking out the window
at the stars, I promised God
I would never take credit for
saving anyone again because
I knew it was too big a job
for any little girl.
It was even too big a job for
Tommy or for the missionaries
even though they were adults.
I told my mother that I didn't think
it was too big a job for Jesus though,

and she said, "Jesus *is* the
saving grace of God."
I had no idea what she was
talking about except that God
was in charge of saving.
She said, yes, God was in charge
of saving, and God put us in charge
of being kind to other people,
and not only being kind, but being
helpful without being fussy.
And another thing, she said,
God put us in charge of remembering
that God was in charge.
Do the missionaries know that?
I asked.
She shook her head like she
always did when she couldn't
believe I'd said whatever
it was I'd said.
You don't have to worry about
what the missionaries know or
don't know, she said.
Remember, you're in charge of
remembering that God's in charge,
and that's a big job that will
last a lifetime.

SOUL STAINS

❧❧❦❦

I thought King James was a friend of King Jesus
until my brother told me King James was a "version."
I told him I knew Mary was a version,
but I didn't know King James was.
VIRGIN, he said, Mary was a VIRGIN.
Since he seemed to be in such a bad mood,
I told him I didn't care who was a version
and who wasn't; I just needed to memorize
the Twenty-third Psalm, King James Version,
and I needed to do it by next Sunday.
I started to walk away, but he grabbed my arm
and made me stay while he took his own sweet
time to tell me what I wanted to know.
VERSION! he yelled, KING JAMES VERSION!!!
I told him it didn't make any difference
whether he whispered softly or screamed
to high heaven; I still didn't know
what a "version" was.
He loosened his grip on my arm and took
a very deep breath and said in slow motion
that "a . . . version . . . is . . . one . . . person's . . .
story . . . about . . . what . . . happened."
When I started to speak,
he put his hand over my mouth,

and asked me if I remembered
digging up the cat we had buried.
Since I couldn't answer with his hand
over my mouth, I had two choices:
Bite his hand or nod.
I decided to "be ye kind."
I nodded up and down. Yes, of course,
I remembered digging up the cat.
Well, he said, when *he* told the story
about digging up the cat, that was
the King Tommy Version, however, when
I told about digging up the cat, that
was the Ann-Is-A-Tattletale Version.
Since he was obviously still in a bad mood,
I went in search of somebody who wasn't.
I went in search of Gladys.
When anybody asked me why I called
my mother by her first name,
I would say because my brother did, and
he would say, because my father did.
Our little sister called her Mama;
we didn't know why.
Our little brother was a baby
and didn't call her anything.

Gladys was in the kitchen polishing
the sin out of the silver.
On the stove each of the four burners
was covered by a pot rattling with steam.
The kitchen fan whirred in concert
with the clattering of the pots.
I smelled turnip greens and sweet potatoes
and meat loaf which must be in the oven.

I saw biscuit dough all ready to be cut,
and gravy brimming over the side
of one of the pots. I suspected
that tapioca was in the other one.
Gladys's face was red, and her hair
was damp and wispy from the steam,
and I wondered if I should wait to
ask about the King James Version,
but when she saw me, she smiled
that smile that said she was
happy to see me, that smile that
said whatever was upsetting her,
I was not the cause.
I hoped it was my brother.
I started to tell her that my brother
was acting mean, but remembered
the Ann-Is-A-Tattletale Version,
and decided against it. Instead I
asked about the King James Version.
It was then I learned that
Jesus was not an American.
Not only was he not an American,
he wasn't even a Presbyterian.
He was a Jew, and didn't speak English.
When King James came along,
which was a long time after Jesus,
he commanded some men to write
the Bible in English, and that's
why we have it today!
Gladys wiped her hands on her apron,
and told me to stir the tapioca,
while she went to get her King James Version.
When she returned, and had checked to be

sure the tapioca hadn't burned,
I learned how to spell "version."

I sat in the living room with the King James
Version, and began to memorize:
"The Lord is my Shepherd. . . ."
My brother and sister were reading books.
The baby was taking a very long nap.
My mother said that church always
wore him out.
My father wasn't home from church yet.
We were all waiting for him to bring
the funny papers.
But we waited and waited and waited. . . .

My mother's eyes were full of tears
she didn't want us to see.
She muttered something about
peeling onions, that it always
made her cry, and dabbed at her eyes
with a Kleenex too small for the job.
She told us she hated to go ahead
with lunch without our father,
but that he was going to be late
because of an unexpected meeting.
My brother asked why was the
Session meeting on Sunday,
which was a dead giveaway that
he had been eavesdropping when our
father had called. I, of course, was happy
that he would be in trouble,
but my mother didn't seem to be in
a mood to reprimand, and simply said

that something had come up.
I didn't know why a Session meeting
after church was all that bad,
especially for our father, because he was
the head of the whole big church, but
something in my mother's voice worried me.

Somehow the funny papers weren't so funny
that day, but we got on our tummies
anyway and spread the papers out on
the floor and read them, all the time
trying to listen to what our father was
saying to our mother.
Ready? my brother asked. Ready, I said,
and my little sister said it, too.
Ready, set, go! We all rolled over; the
papers remained on the floor in order.
The one on the end always had to keep
rolling until he or she was on the other side.
It was a great system; nobody had to get up
when we were ready to switch funny papers.
On that Sunday, however, my brother rolled
just a little bit closer to the door, but
he still couldn't hear what Daddy and Gladys
were saying about the meeting at church.

On a May evening down in Tennessee,
the bedroom doors were not closed
so we could all catch the breeze
of the open windows.
May 4, 1941. . . .
I fought sleep, straining to hear
the whispers that rose and fell,

rose and fell, rose and fell. . . .
Something about war . . .
something about peace . . .
something about the sermon . . .
something about a resolution . . .
whatever that was! . . .
don't preach about war . . .
anymore . . . anymore. . . .
I awoke to the sun smack in my eyes.
I squinted and turned away from the glare.
My brother was standing in the doorway,
his finger over his mouth, telling me to
sh-h-h even though I hadn't said a word.
S-h-h-h! he said again even though
I still had not spoken.
He told me then that Daddy was in big trouble.
I didn't know how a daddy could be in trouble.
I thought only children could get in trouble.
How could a daddy be in trouble?
Especially our Daddy who never caused
any trouble . . . anytime . . . to anybody.
My brother said that the men had a meeting,
and told my Daddy he couldn't preach
about war anymore.
My brother heard Gladys say that
my father didn't preach about war . . .
he preached about peace. . . .
My father said he preached the Gospel
as he understood it.
It's not about war, he said. It's about Jesus.
When we got down to breakfast,
we said the blessing, and then our father
told us he didn't want us to worry,

but he was having a little difficulty.
I said that we knew about it already, and
my brother said that I didn't know anything.
Well, my father said, that's why he wanted
to talk to us, because sometimes people talk
about things they know nothing about.
Sometimes people start rumors, he said,
and it hurts other people.
He said he wanted us to know the facts
in case anybody said anything to us.
I could tell this was going to be
a long conversation, and I didn't know
whether I could eat my oatmeal or not.
I looked around to see if anybody else
was eating their oatmeal and my father
said, Ann, I want you to hear this,
so I guessed I couldn't eat my oatmeal,
but my mother said, yes, that what
our father had to say was very important,
but maybe we could eat our breakfast
while we talked.
My father said, of course, and smiled at me.
Then he said that actually he was a
little hungry himself, and my mother said
that was a good sign, and we all laughed
and began to eat and listen.
That's how we found out that people
in the church were mad at my father,
that, and the phone calls on that Monday
after our father preached Peace.
A prominent banker had called a meeting
to discuss getting rid of my father.
Behind his back, my mother said.

On Monday morning a man who worked
at the bank called to cancel the baptism
of his baby that was scheduled for next week.
It was not more than an hour later when
a bride called to say she wouldn't be wanting
our father to conduct her wedding service.
A while later a man called to say he liked
my father, but he owed $80,000 to the bank,
and he couldn't afford to offend the banker.
By Thursday I knew the entire Twenty-third
Psalm, King James Version and practiced
saying it in front of the mirror when I wasn't
answering the phone.
My mother always told me I had to be seven
before I could answer the phone, but she was
tired of the phone "ringing off the hook."
Two months before my seventh birthday,
I was allowed to answer the phone.
Every time it rang, my mother ran out
the back door, so I wouldn't have to tell
a lie when I said she wasn't home.
One day I answered the phone and Mrs. Dunaway,
in her cracky voice, said,
"Tell your father I said, 'Bless his soul.'"
When I told him, he said he needed
somebody to bless his soul.
He was already tired of the bickering,
and it had only been five days.
I asked my mother why my father
needed somebody to bless his soul,
and she said because no matter what he did,
somebody criticized him, and he was just
trying to be Christian.

So I said, in the Twenty-third Psalm, King James
Version, is this: "He restoreth my soul."
Go tell your father, she said.
So I did and he said he was grateful.
On Friday night we went to the B&W Cafeteria,
and I had vegetable soup and baked custard and
then we went to the movies, and got popcorn.
We need a little fun after this difficult week,
my mother said.
On Saturday, my father worked in the yard
for hours, and then came in and said he was
wonderfully tired, and he thought he could
sleep well tonight.
My mother said she was at the typewriter all day
writing a short story, and "blessedly forgetting
about all this mess," and she was wonderfully tired,
too, but not too tired to make hot fudge sauce to
pour over our ice cream. A very special treat!
On Sunday I recited the Twenty-third Psalm,
King James Version, without one mistake.
Mrs. Dunaway said, "Upon my soul!"
and hugged me to her bosom which was covered
in scratchy lace her mother had sent her
from Belgium years ago.

What we didn't learn around the dining-
room table came to us little by little,
day by day, month after month,
in the whispers of the night.
My mother's voice blended with my father's,
and the stories were told and our prayers
were said. "Now I lay me down to sleep.
I pray the Lord my soul to keep.

If I should die before I wake,
I pray the Lord my soul to take."
One night my father said that wasn't
his favorite prayer because it taught
little children to think about
their own souls, but nobody else's.
I liked it because it rhymed.
But I added: Bless Gladys and Daddy
and Tommy and Bill and Jane and Dan-Dan,
and Grandmother and Grandfather and all my
aunts and uncles and cousins and friends. Amen.
My father said that was much better.
I can also say the Twenty-third Psalm,
King James Version, I said.
My father said, Go ahead, so I did.

Some of the people in the church
called my father names and my brother
said we should beat them up,
but my father said there's not going to be
any of that sort of talk around this house.
Then he told us that Jesus said forgive those
who persecute you and speak all manner
of evil against you for my sake.
Then he went into his study and
listened to a recording of organ music.
We could hear him humming all the way outside.

When my father told my mother that he was
being criticized for preaching racial equality,
my mother said she wasn't surprised.
She also wasn't surprised that the businessmen
were angry because he preached about higher

wages for the poor.
My mother said, "Let's go to the beach."
So we did.

Sunday morning at the beach is very strange.
Instead of my bathing suit, I wore a dress
and felt sand in my patent leather shoes.
My Daddy wore a suit.
My mother said she was on vacation.
So did the others.
I wanted to go to church because the only
time I could sit with my father in church
was when we were on vacation.
When the minister said a long prayer,
my father put his head in his hands.
I looked at him out of the corner of my eye.
I wondered if he was asking God to
restore his soul.
When he sang, he sang loudly
just the way he did at the Hymnsings.
On the way home I asked him if his
soul was restored.
He said God was always restoring his soul.
He said he hoped I understood that
he had to be faithful to his calling.
So he had to preach what he thought was
the Gospel of Jesus Christ.
I wish I could preach something that
would make everybody happy, he said,
but I have to preach what I think is right.
I have to preach what I think God
wants me to preach.
It's very hard sometimes, he said.

I have to be sure in my heart that
it's about Jesus and not about me.
It's not when I'm resting that I feel peaceful;
it's when I feel I've been faithful.
I can't be the minister of a church where
I'm asked not to preach what I believe is true.
Do you understand that? he asked.
Not really, I said. I'm only seven years old.
The only thing I really understand is
that it's about Jesus.
That's enough, he said. That's really enough.
It's all about Jesus, the grace of God.